THE WAYS I TRIED TO CALL YOU HOME

First printing 2025
Published by Double Text Media
Long Beach, CA
www.doubletextmedia.com

ISBN: 979-8-9913662-0-5

For you.

Table of Contents

All of the other loves were poisoned from the inside

Blackened gums and rotted hearts, we
cut the bones to try to save the rest of the body but couldn't, or
didn't, either way we buried the scraps in the earth behind us.
Either way, we told new stories about the old scars and
forgot the stories were new and the scars were old, we
got back to some new version of our old selves,
half-hearted and then all the way, like our lives depended on
it and they did, they really did. Now my ex lovers are
just ex lovers, off somewhere in the world
kissing other people and never thinking of me,
like I am to them what they have become to me, memory
mixed with something sweet and Vaseline to blur the edges.
No one is wrong anymore, we are all
over everything and we all smile in new Christmas card
photos on other people's fridges and stay
quiet in the kitchens of our own homes. I
remember believing that love could never be boring, or
selfish, and I was so wrong then. I once
thought love was some whole, grand thing, an
umbrella meant to shield me from all my own
vices, the unhealed wishes I wanted to let
wash all over me, furious in pastel like a child banging mallets on a
xylophone, like I could never have too much of anything, even
you, especially you. So go ahead and leave me in that untouchable
zone, the corner of your mind you tell yourself is gone.

Because this is a love story, I will start at the beginning

and end in the middle of wherever we go from here.
I won't finish the thought, I won't close my lips
around the last sound of your name just yet.
Because this is a love story, my mouth
will only remember the first kiss,
and a few after that, but especially the first one
ankle deep in the Pacific Ocean and laughing
about how we made our love like movie stars
before the cameras stopped rolling.
And because this is a love story,
the cameras will not stop rolling

until, of course, you want them to.
But this is a love story, so I know you'll call me back
to life soon, and I will have a new dress
and the same problems, and you will have the new shirt
I picked out for you at the thrift store,
the one that you swore you wouldn't wear
until you tried it on and thought *wow,*
with you I could be anything,
you will make me anything.

And this is a love story
so I will become something to you,
a mother, a wife, or a glimmer
of one past summer when you almost became
everything you've ever wanted to be.

When I tell this story later, I skip to the end.

You walk into our relationship with a wandering heart,
and my first chore is to catch it.

Before long,
I am taking all my plants out of their pots
and digging them into the ground.
I let the roots stretch long
so when you walk outside,
before you go anywhere else,
you are surrounded by a garden of us.

You leave the front door locked,
or unlocked, or cracked,
but never wide open.
You can always leave
but you don't.

Your father leaves town for the weekend
and we call his kitchen ours.
I burn a candle at the high top table
and you try on the taste of calling me your wife.

This is not a game but we are playing.
I tell you another girl in our bed will rot the wood of our love,
but I kiss them at parties when I know you're watching,
and sometimes when you aren't.

My high school boyfriend sends a letter to our mailbox
and I do not love him, but I keep the envelope.
I kiss the first girl you almost left me for,
in another dark kitchen full of glass bottles.

I want to touch everything that doesn't remind you of me.
When I love anything that isn't you, you swallow the keys.

I make a campsite home
of every new apartment. I do your laundry.
We laugh about how together,
we can wash a whole load of just turquoise and teal.
I separate our clothes into black, blue,
and everything else.

Every time I change,
I call it healing and you call it changing.
We are both right.

I walk farther away from who I was when we started
and I am trying to drag you with me.
I am trying to pull the key from your throat to keep us here.
I am in the house, but I look out every window
for new faces on the street
when you turn your back to me.

When you leave me for the most obvious girl,
this is the only part of the story I tell.
I leave everything that reminds me of you
in a trash bag at your feet on your father's porch.
I blow out the candles.
I pretend I never lived here.

If you've ever been in love

you know just how elastic
the human brain can be.
How we stretch around a bad thing
and call it good.

And then,
how it becomes good
because we say so.

We know how to believe
in anything.
A god, a promise,

a future of rose petals
pressed to my tongue,
stuck to the bottom of my feet
as I walk to you.

The way we make
the truth
a meter,
a mile.

The way a shoe pulls
bubble gum
half a city block long.

The way we turn
everything into more
than it is,

and then
less.

on playing house

When we moved in,
new and high on untested love,
we painted every wall
with tubes of lipstick
I found at the bottom of my purse
and I cried when the nub of my favorite color
wore down to the bullet
but now it's on the wall.

It's the color of cranberry bruise,
of blood dust
and rotting roses.
It reminds me of us.
That makes this room my favorite room
and this house my favorite house.

We should have painted the door's lips
so we could pretend to be swallowed
like little jelly beans
every time we walk in,
and spit out like gum balls
every time we leave.

We could still do that,
it's not too late.
Ghosts could still settle
into the bones,
bend the staircase
into a new spine, and we could
let the whole thing stand on its own.

And if that happens,
then this home will walk away
wearing my favorite lipstick and I'll miss it.
I'll miss it,
but I'll let you go.

Wendy Darling

Every woman I've ever loved has lost herself to someone. A father, a lover, a child who will grow up to repeat the pattern. We always said we wouldn't let that happen, that I would always have time to write and you would sometimes do the grocery shopping. But here we are now, you are watching television and I am making dinner. You are with your friends and I am folding the laundry. I ask for help and you promise to try, your words as empty as the fridge when I come home from a weekend away. You yell about how tired you are, about the bills you have to pay, as though we do not share them. You will hate me for saying this, but you are just like your father. You were raised to believe that men are above domestic work, so now your time is too valuable to spend it meal planning. You will deny this belief, though it lives so deeply in your bones it is indistinguishable from the marrow. And so we'll break every promise we made to ourselves. I will shoulder every shared responsibility, lie awake at night worried about our children's after school schedules, the cobwebs in the corner of the bathroom, my own day job, and you will sleep. You will become more like yourself, and I will become less. One day you will meet someone who reminds you of the person I was, before all of this. You will kiss her and say it's because you miss me. You will leave the same way you came, and I will have nothing to show for it.

I have been here before

Not at this old oak table
and not with you, my sweet love
but with others.

We are fighting.
You are sitting across from me
asking questions
I do not want to answer.

And for the first time
I can see all the coffee stains on your teeth,
the way they match the yellow of your eyes.
And I think

I have been here before.
This is what every love becomes.
You are just like everyone else.

Apology

I have stopped writing poetry.
I watch the most stunning sunset I have ever seen
reflect in the rare, shallow salt water of the desert floor,
and no words come to mind.

I watch my nephew find his hands,
recognize me for the first time,
and I don't write about it.

I am cementing the floodgates.
I've got all my fingers in the dam.
You and I are *cordial*, peaceful

so long as I float taut on the surface
like a lily pad for you to walk on.
I wish I could say you looked at me once,

you said one thing,
we had one fight,
but the truth is we drifted here.

We thought we knew the way home,
so we turned the navigation off
and no one wants to be the first to say it.

You're not lost,
but I will be.

I have stopped asking for what I need.
After years of hearing me, you've stopped.
Half of me hates you, the other half knows
I break every good thing in due time.

I have stopped writing poetry because
I have stopped telling the truth,
and so have you.
We hold our breath,
hoping that if we stay quiet enough
the ghosts will pass through
and onto the next home.
That we'll inhale unhaunted and
want the same things again.

Forgive me, I still remember believing in miracles.
Forgive me, it is almost time to go.

Tell me again about that one time you almost became everything you've ever wanted to be.

Tell me again about the self doubt your father planted in you when you were a child that you keep watering, even now. About the ex girlfriend you wanted a forever with even though she never believed in any of your dreams. Tell me about your dreams. The ones where staircases fold into cars without steering wheels or emergency brakes. Tell me about the ones where I meet your mother and she loves me. Tell me about the ones where you come home from work and I am here, barefoot and ready for you. Tell me about all your favorite movies, the ones with sad boys who realize they've been in love with the wrong girl all this time. Tell me how afraid you are that you've been in love with the wrong girl all this time. Tell me how the future could have been if you'd become a teacher or an artist instead of whatever it is you do now. You could have been something, I know. Tell me again about the first time you saw fireflies in Baltimore, and were disappointed by how dim and fleeting their lights were. Tell me again about the first time you held my hand in Los Angeles and thought my city wasn't as shiny as it looks in the movies. Tell me again how everything you thought you wanted tasted better when you drank it from someone else's mouth.

Breakup! at the Disco

after Micah Bournes

The concert is over and we are walking the long road
back to the Vegas hotel instead of taking the tram
because we are on the hunt for a little more time.

We are watching the sky fall, sharing one more drink,
queen and king of this hologram for one more moment.

We know it is over, that this was always going to end.
From the first date, the first lie, the first secondhand lover,
there are only two ways these things can go.

It's been three years, and each one
has felt more impossible than the next,
no air to breathe, and more nightmares than daylight.

But in the beginning, I was too young to know
that love could be different from that.

I thought you would change but you didn't.
I know now that you could set yourself on fire,
but you'd never learn.

This is also true of me. For us,
I would have become a fucking arsonist.
I would have sat at a table for two,
looking lonely for so many more years.

I would have made a home of this house of memories,
haunted from the very beginning.
I would have pulled my heart out of my chest
just to show you, and I would not have asked for more.

What an expense, my happily ever after
for the cut of your love.
A butter knife death.

I wouldn't ever try to make you leave.
I'd keep us on the tightrope
until the colors turned to gray.

I would have weathered every downtown storm,
every fire sign of yours.

I would have tried to love all the things
you hate about yourself. I would have lost my mind
in a wedding gown. I would have stayed
until all the guests at the party followed the ghosts out.

But now there's no you and me,
so welcome to the end of eras.

We are holding our breath.
We are trying to stay still,
upside down with a perfect view.

We are still sunbathing on a beachfront of bad blood.
You smile even though you're sad.

I know you're thinking about someone else,
but I haven't let the fantasy go yet.
At night in my dreams,
I swear that I'll always paint you golden,
and you call me your double bubble disco queen.

In my dreams, we are all inside jokes and champagne.
But here, when the sun comes up,
we are cocaine and gasoline.

We are sycophants on velvet sofas
worshiping different people,
two sinners, a dynasty decapitated,
waves swallowing each other,
heroes no one will remember.

I don't know it yet, but soon I'll be sitting pretty
in my brand new scars.
Next Christmas will be warm
without your broken light eyes.

Soon, this will be a night that time forgot,
so far away that I don't write about you anymore.
The ice will melt back to life, and I will be fine.

It's a hell of a feeling, to let us fade away,
to let the memory turn to stone.
I'll look back and wonder who I was trying to be.
I don't know yet that past lovers will always haunt me,
that being a poet means being blue
will always be better than being over it,
that your fantasies will become your legacy,
your kinks showing up in new love's knots.

I don't know yet that one day,
you'll have been gone so long
I'll forget what you feel like.
That I'll feel so normal
that you just disappear.

I'll never know if you remember me
in the same way as I remember you.
If you can see my face in the pictures.

For now, we will love until it's not.
We will try to finish the daydream.

We will promise each other a place in the pile of Polaroids,
leave no liquor on the shelf,
watch the water fall over our reflections,
let it all move right through us
until we feel alright. [1]

---

[1] This poem includes 67 references to the Panic! at the Disco album *Death of a Bachelor*.

I leave a trail of breadcrumbs

so I can find my way back
to where I came from.
I came from a body
of breadcrumbs.
I leave a trail
of my body
so I can find my way back.
I leave my body
so I can find my way back.
I find my way back
to my body
in pieces pressed
into the carpet
or, I don't
find my way back
to where I came from
and you find a line
of space dust
winding from
room to room
and it sticks
to the soles
of your shoes
and you think of me
and wonder
what we could
have been if only
we'd followed the path
back home.

Happy Early Birthday

I left my deranged little dream
scribbled into the square
of your birthday on your calendar.
Have you found it yet?
I promise it is not a prayer,
it is not a wish I made for you,
it was just a dream.
I relieve myself of wishing
on your stars.
I gave them all back to you
with the book I borrowed
and didn't read.

My last wish is that you find it,
months from now, though I don't know
if I can wait that long.
Would it ruin everything
if I told you to look today?
Should I leave something unfinished
to come back to? Will you think of me
in six months, when you flip the page
and see the last thing I gave you?
Will you know it was me?
Will you remember?

the forgetting season

I pay $400/month in rent to my friend's boyfriend for a little room with two windows that let in too much light at night. The streetlights must be brand new but I won't be here long enough to justify buying new curtains or drilling holes in the new walls. I sleep on a twin size trundle bed I borrowed from my parents. I have a shower caddy and a calendar. Everything else is stacked in boxes in my childhood bedroom. This is temporary. My roommates are nice, but they are in love and I am not, so when they invite me downstairs to watch tv on the couch with them, I decline. I cocoon in my trundle bed, watching sitcoms on a tiny screen or writing bad poems. I go to work every day and I do not decorate my cubicle. I water my boss's peace lily, lower her window shade halfway in the afternoon so the leaves don't burn. I drink warm green tea from the same cup all day. It is bitter and keeps me awake at night but I think I'm getting thinner. I go to the gym every night, run on the same treadmill, push my tired body against the same machines. I have smoothies or cereal for dinner. I am mostly happy but I am not well. I fill my belly with tequila and sleep on my best friend's couch every Saturday night. Everyone is so good to me. I am still lonely in my fervent discipline. I can't remember the last summer we were not in love.

My laughter is contagious

When you leave, your belly will bubble
with giggle for weeks on end.
I leave lipstick on everything.
You'll wake up and find me printed on you
like we've just made neat and perfect love.
Like there is such a thing as that.
My heartbreak is infectious.
You'll find my hurt rattling around
in your own chest after I'm gone.
And when you look up at the moon,
you'll think of how my ex lover might be looking
at the same moon with someone else,
and you'll feel something, even though
you've never met. I'm like that.
A snake shedding my skin everywhere I go.
A magnet trying to push one face of myself
away from the other.

For J.

I see what you were talking about with all the coffee spoons
and measuring your days with them.
I wish I could stack all of mine

neat and nested into each other like lovers,
and watch the tower grow taller and taller
but I have to wash them.

I could measure my year in dishwasher pods
because I have a dishwasher now,
but those dissolve behind closed doors.

I could measure my life in dead house plants,
in rotted fruit,
in candles burned down to the glass.

I could pile everything I've ever consumed
into one heap and call it art.

You could see it in a museum:
Girl measures her life without coffee spoons.
Medium: everything she's ever burned through.

When we joke about the zombie apocalypse until you promise you'll kill me if I get bit

what I hear
is when you think of the end of the world,
we are not bandaging each other's wounds.

I die in the first act, a tragic thread
of the backstory you'll tell
your one true post apocalyptic lover someday.
You are the main character,
and you only have one gun.

You grew up watching movies with men
who made it to the end days alone and so
when you imagine the end of the world,
I'm not there.

The difference between us
is I would never want to survive
the kind of apocalypse you love to read about.
But if I did, I would keep you alive.

I would try. I'd slide raw beef
under the locked bathroom door
to keep you with me. I'd fall in love
with the small hope
that might bring the old you back to me,
but I'd learn the new you.

The difference between us
is that even now, years after
I fell out of my hollow little love,
I don't want to live in a world
where you don't exist.

I am happy to know that somewhere,
someone else hears you laugh every day.
Somewhere, you are at the grocery store
buying turkey breasts and spinach.
The peppers in your garden are growing
and you are dreaming of some bright future,
a wife who takes your children to church on Sundays.

I know it is easier to have love for you
when I do not know you.
I know I love you alone.
I know you don't see me in every airport you pass through.
You do not think about my grocery lists.

The world has not ended, but still,
I am gone.

every heavy thing

I learned you like something between a god
and a lab sample, a test subject. I mean,
I was once a pious scientist
in the etymology of you.

If you knew yourself like the back of your hand,
I knew you like a go-to karaoke song,
ever changing in color and meaning
as the years go by.
But we didn't have years.

Do you remember how instead of your last name,
I took on every heavy thing
you asked me to hold for you?
Your exhaustion after a long work shift,
your errands,
the way your father loved your sister
more than he loved you.

My heart became a purse full of rocks,
a pillowcase filled with every word
you couldn't take back.
Every small apology, a chance
to bend myself into every shape I thought you wanted
until I looked so much like your shadow,
you forgot me entirely.

I am writing to tell you

I don't want to write poems to ghosts,
but I do. I am writing to tell you
you were wrong about me,
you turned your head too soon
and didn't see me catch the light.
You didn't see me shine but if you had,
you would have stayed.
I am writing to tell you
I am more than what you remember.
I am writing to tell you
I wish you thought about me
the way I think about you.
I am writing to tell you
that all of my poems are about ghosts.
I am writing to tell you that you are a ghost
and I see you everywhere.
Every time I open a new door I think
maybe you'll be there,
sitting and waiting for me
the way you've never been.
I am writing to tell you
that I've never made a space
you couldn't fill, never wrapped a sheet
around a bed you couldn't warm.
I am writing to tell you
you will always be here.
You will always be something to me.

Codependence

On nights like these, when I ache to be young
and unhealed again, I have to face how good it felt
to get lost in other people.

The way the body misses the rocking of the boat
when you reach land again. The way you crave
hunger when you've eaten too much.

The way I turned every mirror to frosted glass
by crawling into the mouth of someone
who could swallow me whole
and watching their breath fog up my reflection.

Most days, now, I would not choose this.
But after dusk, I would be lying if I told you that leaving
my ugliest parts in someone else's closet
wasn't sometimes worth leaving the rest of me too.

Still, even on the good nights,
I remember the pull,
the all-consuming sickness
of being so wrapped up in someone else
I never had to feel alone.

Only ever incomplete or with my lover,
famine or fight, too much
or nothing at all.

Addendum to Codependence

[Some nights, I do indulge the ghost,
the echo of my old self.
I read all 37 of your wife's Google reviews
looking for some intimate truth of you between the lines.

You are not the only sand I've buried by head in,
not the only welcome I have overstayed.
But your poison was the sweetest and now,
when I think of you for too long, I forget myself

or, I remember us collapsing on each other
like a single dead star.
See, I began writing a poem about myself,
and still, I got lost in you.]

Edge of the Earth

"You push me in circles to the edge of the earth. But I can't go any further
til I start coming back to you" - Beaches

Maybe the earth pulls the apple to its own core,
but you do not think about me.

The same world is spinning around us
but we aren't in the same circles.

I am not a piece of fruit on your planet. We are the same size,
whether we be peaches, oceans, or asteroids.

There is nothing natural about the way I return to you,
over and over. It feels innate but I've made it up.

I come back to you like a revolving door, a carousel with no children
and only me, holding on and waiting to catch a glimpse
that will have to last me until the next go around.

I have to let you go now

[I have to stop believing you'll be behind every new door I open. I have to stop wishing I could call you. I have to stop writing poems about you. My poet friends say it's ok to write about the same thing over and over if you're working something out, it just means there is something there you haven't dug all the way up, but I have buried and unburied you so many times you are unrecognizable. I have toxic relationships with all of my muses, but especially with you because you are gone. There is too much space between the real truth and the one I believe about you. The truth is, you are someone else now and if we met for lunch, I'd be comfortable and bored. What I believe is that if we met for lunch, we'd fall madly back in love and we'd run away together or we'd just melt into one single candle flame. It would be so pure and bright and loud and undeniable that everyone else would write poems about how we found our way back to each other and they'd be right to call us lucky and true. I don't have to bury you. You are just some person, clocking into work every morning and living your life a thousand miles away and never thinking of me. I have to bury my version of you, frantic and fantastical and nothing like the man you are.]

but I don't want to.

Addendum II to Codependence

There is an alternate universe in which I believed your words
more than your hands.
In which you said you didn't love me
and I iced my own bruised heart
somewhere else without you.

In which we came back together as friends a few years later,
kind and glad to know each other again.
In which I did not set fire
to all the good little things about us.

I can see now that we do not remember each other
the same way.
You are nostalgia thick and tacky as honey
in the valves of my heart.

You are all of my unfinished business,
a loop I wish I could close that still opens
wide-mouthed into the future and the past.
I am the one stuck on that merry go-round,
I am the one coming back to see
what new thing we could build
and finding everything except for you.

I am obsessed with something made up.
I am addicted to remembering you wrong.

I have never known rage like yours.
after Emily Dickinson

You come from a long line of angry men
and I am the hard stop,
exclamation point knocked into italics
but still holding my own. Who's there?
I know you by your voice
but I want to hear you say it.
I want to hear you become
something unknown to me.

You will call and call and call and I
will not answer like I used to.
We have done this before,
on bright summer days
and alone in the dark,
but I will fold you away now.

I will tuck everything I have of you in a box
and leave it in the dirt somewhere.
You can look all you want, but I'll forget
where I left it and I won't go searching.
We've come to the end.
I must go in, the fog is rising.

What you don't say

when you text me four years later to tell me
you swear you saw me hiking by a river in Seattle this afternoon
is that you know it wasn't me.
Or, that you see me everywhere
and couldn't hold that in any longer.
You needed me to know.
What we don't say
is that the last time we spoke we were screaming,
taking a wrecking ball to every wall we built for each other.
Or, we were soft and sad.
I do not remember the final goodbye now,
only that every time felt like it wouldn't be the last,
and it wasn't.
We don't talk about the blocked phone numbers
and midnight calls,
or the time we watched a horror movie
and I drove back to my apartment at 3am
instead of sleeping over.
We don't talk about the ways I tried to call you home.
We don't talk about how it's your 2 year wedding anniversary,
and you're still looking for my face
in every stranger at the river.

Almost

They say close only counts
in horseshoes and hand grenades,
but what about situationships?
What about engagement rings
that never make it to the wedding aisle,
the *what ifs* on the other side
of weird timing and wrong choices?

What about all of our almosts?
The way I spent a short lifetime believing
that we just might make it, grow old together
and retire by the beach, or raise kids,
or fight over everything for eight long years
until we both gave up
and set fire to something that was real once.
Now I'm supposed to act like it didn't happen,
because it didn't.

But you know these poems aren't really about you.

They're about the things we almost were.
The way that once, I would have chosen you
over everything, moved two states away from home
and forgotten my own last name.
The way we are strangers to each other now.
I am writing about the ways I remember you in this new life.
I am writing about the near-miss,
ships passing, two car mirrors kissing on the freeway.
I am writing about driving through the tulip fields
ten days before they all bloomed
and flying home flowerless.
I am writing about a hurricane turning over its shoulder
and missing a whole city,
a razor grazing a neck.
I am writing about the echo of the alarm
announcing a tornado that never touches down.
An asteroid sliding past our atmosphere.
I am writing about the way we were just so close.

Beyond the Book

The Ways I Tried to Call You Home has an official playlist! Find it, and more, by visiting doubletextmedia.com/#twittcyh or by scanning the QR code below.

Acknowledgements

Thank you to *Anti-Heroin Chic,* who published an earlier version of "Tell me again about that one time you almost became everything you've ever wanted to be."

Thank you to my writing group, Nick Rada, Kendall McClellan, and Evan Chelsee. Without your guidance and support, this book would have never seen the light of day. Thank you to Valerie Nies and Ryan Stevens for reading earlier versions of this collection. Thank you to my creative writing club at work; many of these poems started in our 15 minute writing sprints.

Thank you to the loved ones who graciously listen to me process the same things over and over as many times as I need to. I am endlessly grateful for your patience. Without you, I would never heal from anything.

Thank you to Sidney for the loving and supportive home we have built together.

And finally, one more thank you to Evan. Making things with you is one of the greatest joys of my life. Let's never stop.

About the Author

Christina Brown is a poet and podcaster living in Long Beach, CA. She is the cohost of The Bi Pod: A Queer Podcast. Her work has appeared in The Los Angeles Press, A Moon of One's Own, The Sunshine Lounge, Ink & Marrow, and other venues. In her free time, you'll find her reading niche non-fiction books, trying not to kill her houseplants, and never getting over anything. She is the author of two poetry collections, *Girl Teeth* (innateDIVINITYpress) and *The Ways I Tried to Call You Home* (Double Text Media).

Instagram: @christina.leigh.brown

www.ingramcontent.com/pod-product-compliance
Lightning Source LLC
Chambersburg PA
CBHW050449150626
46551CB00029B/2306